DOWN ON THE FARM

Designed and Pieced by

LESLEY BRANKIN

Quilted by

Jan Chandler
(Quilting Solutions)

Happy Quilting!

Lesley Brankin

An intermediate/advanced level project using
Foundation Piecing techniques

CONTENTS

Materials 3
Choosing Fabric 4
Making up the Blocks 4
Assembling the Quilt 5
Inner Sashing 9
Pieced Borders 9
Outer Sashing 9
Quilting 9
Binding 10
Finishing 10

General Techniques 11
- Quarter Square Triangle Block
- Plaited Tail
- Tassel Tail

Foundation Piecing - a Brief Guide 12

	Guidance Notes	Colour Plate	Templates
Bull	14	25	27
Cat	14	24	28
Cockerel	15	26	29
Collie Dog	15	24	30
Cow	16	25	31
Donkey	16	25	32
Drake	17	25	33
Duck	17	25	34
Goat	18	24	35
Goose	18	24	36
Farmer	19	23	37-38
Hen	19	26	39
Hills	19	23	40
Horse	20	25	41
House	20	23	42-43
Path	20	23	44
Pig	21	26	45
Rabbit	21	26	46
Sheep	22	24	47
Turkey	22	26	48

Disclaimer

Every care has been taken to ensure the accuracy of these instructions, but no guarantee can be given with regard to the finished quilt as materials and procedures used will necessarily vary.

Finished Dimensions: 61" x 61"

This quilt is made from many different fabrics, many used in small quantities. The nature of foundation piecing techniques makes it difficult to give precise fabric requirements so the following are quite generous quantities. Quantities provided assume standard width (112 cm, 42"/44") wide fabrics

Fabrics for Central Section:

- 0.5 m (⅝ yd) each of pale grey, pale green and pale blue fabrics
- 6, 15 cm (6") widths of purple, blue and turquoise fabrics
- 10 cm (4") magenta fabric for small sashings beside landscape blocks
- 20 cm (8") pink and 20 cm (8") turquoise fabric for inner sashing
- 20 cm (8") pink and 20 cm (8") turquoise fabric for outer sashing

No specific requirements are given for the pieced border as I suggest using left over fabrics from the above sashings and your animal blocks. Why not look through your scrap basket (as I did) if you need a few extra?

Animal Blocks:

- animal prints, landscape prints and fabric scraps*
- background fabrics (included in amounts given above)
- Stitch 'n' Tear or thin paper for paper piecing (e.g. cheap computer paper)
- a variety of ¼" and ⅜" buttons
- perlé embroidery threads

  * If buying fabrics especially, a fat eighth should be enough of a main animal fabric for two 5" or 6" blocks.

Additional Needs:

- neutral sewing thread
- 64" x 64" sized piece of wadding
- 67" x 67" backing fabric (allows for Long Arm quilting)
- 60 cm (24") grass green for double binding
- decorative quilting threads

CHOOSING FABRICS

Choosing fabrics is both great fun and a fundamental step to stamping your own identity on any project. Just because I have chosen to use a specific colour or texture of a fabric does not mean that you are obliged to follow my dictate. Use this design as an opportunity to follow your own creative style and perhaps use up some of that ever-growing stash?

For the backgrounds, I would recommend that you use non-patterned fabrics that will not compete with the animals themselves. Plains or marbles are ideal. The ground cover strips are an ideal chance to indulge in some vibrant or highly patterned designs.

As the animals themselves do not use very much fabric, this offers the 'opportunity' to source specific fabric designs. You may be lucky enough to find some special animal skin prints, however, it is probable that you will have to look for suitable alternatives. Be sure to audition all sorts of patterned and textured fabrics. Does it look like skin, fur, feathers etc?

MAKING UP THE BLOCKS

My suggested order of working is to make all the blocks before you start to construct the full quilt top. However, if you prefer you can of course work one row at a time.

Instructions for each block are given individually, this allows you to use the designs simply as quilt blocks and then use them to create your own quilt and project layouts.

All of the blocks use Foundation Piecing techniques. A brief overview of the technique has been included here (see page 12) or there are many excellent texts available explaining this technique if you are not already familiar with it. The important thing to remember is to always to work in the order given (rather like a painting by numbers set) and to press and trim seams as you go. For ease of use when piecing, I strongly recommend that you always work with generous sized pieces of fabric - if you are too miserly you will find that frustration may rule the day! Likewise allow a generous amount of fabric at the edges of the block - that way you will have plenty of scope when trimming your blocks to their final sizes.

If you are making up my full quilt design you will need to make the appropriate number of blocks for each animal. The block instructions tell you how many of that block to make or you can refer to the quilt construction figure on page 5. When making more than one block for each type of animal, you may wish to do as I did and use a mirrored image for some of the blocks. In this case you will need to transpose the given template patterns using a scanner, carbon paper or ask a copy shop to do this for you.

When trimming your blocks ready to sew together, do make sure they are ½" bigger than the finished size specified. This provides your ¼" seam allowance.

ASSEMBLING THE QUILT

A few hints before you start:

- When cutting background strips you may need to join several smaller lengths of fabric together to make the total width specified - the instructions given refer to the total joined length required.
- For ease of working, you may find it easier to cut sashing and strip lengths just slightly longer than needed - these can then be trimmed as you sew.
- Remember to press seam allowances as you proceed.
- The figure below illustrates the full quilt block layout and should be used as a general reference diagram.

General Block Layout

Row 1

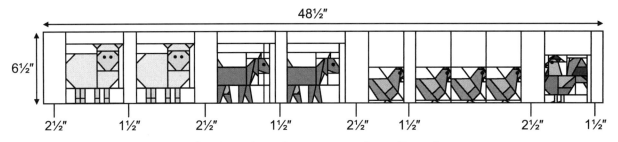

48½"

6½"

2½"   1½"   2½"   1½"   2½"   1½"   2½"   1½"

Cutting sizes for spacer strips - Row 1

1. From pale grey fabric cut 6½" strips:
   - 4 x 1½"
   - 4 x 2½"
2. Join strips and animal blocks as shown above.
3. From pink fabric cut a 48½" x 2½" wide strip. Attach to bottom of joined blocks; see general reference diagram.

Row 2

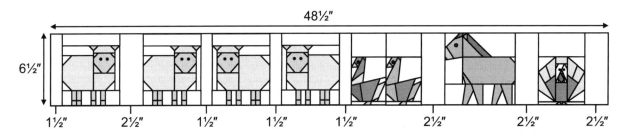

48½"

6½"

1½"   2½"   1½"   1½"   1½"   2½"   2½"   2½"

Cutting sizes for spacer strips - Row 2

1. From pale blue fabric cut 6½" strips:
   - 4 x 1½"
   - 4 x 2½"
2. Join strips and animal blocks as shown above.
3. From purple fabric cut a 48½" x 2½" wide strip. Attach to bottom of joined blocks; see general reference diagram.

Rows 3 and 4

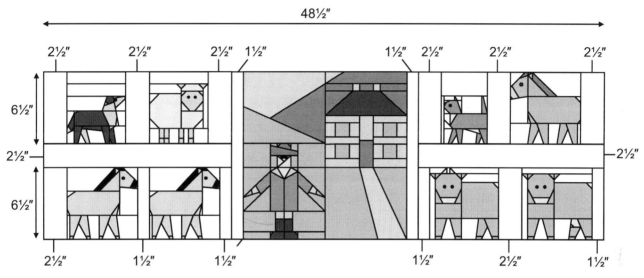

Cutting sizes for spacer strips - Rows 3 & 4

1. From blue fabric cut two 17½" x 2½" strips.
2. From pale green fabric cut 6½" strips:
   - 6 x 2½"
3. Join a dog and a sheep with appropriate strips as shown above.
4. Join a cat and a donkey likewise.
5. Insert a blue fabric strip in between animal strips as shown.

6. From pale grey fabric cut 6½" strips:
   - 4 x 1½"
   - 2 x 1½"
7. Join horses with appropriate strips as shown.
8. Join a bull and a cow likewise.
9. Insert a blue fabric strip in between animal strips as shown.

10. From magenta fabric cut two 14½" x 1½" strips.
11. Join central landscape blocks together as shown.
12. Attach a magenta strip to either side of central block.
13. Add a set of animal blocks to either side of this block.
14. From turquoise fabric cut a 48½" x 2½" wide strip. Attach to bottom of joined blocks; see general reference diagram.

Row 5

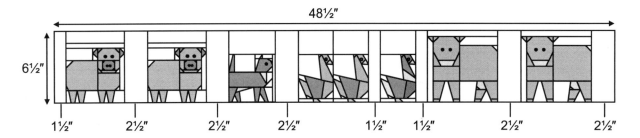

48½"

6½"

1½"   2½"   2½"   2½"   1½"   1½"   2½"   2½"

Cutting sizes for spacer strips - Row 5

1. From pale blue fabric cut 6½" strips:
   - 3 x 1½"
   - 5 x 2½"
2. Join strips and animal blocks as shown above.
3. From blue fabric cut a 48½" x 2½" wide strip. Attach to bottom of joined blocks; see general reference diagram.

Row 6

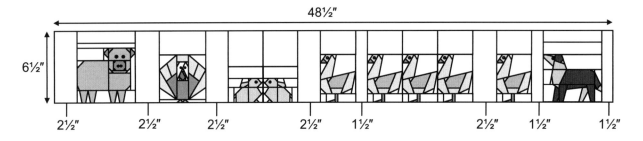

48½"

6½"

2½"   2½"   2½"   2½"   1½"   2½"   1½"   1½"

Cutting sizes for spacer strips - Row 6

1. From pale blue fabric cut 6½" strips:
   - 3 x 1½"
   - 5 x 2½"
2. Join strips and animal blocks as shown above.
3. From purple fabric cut a 48½" x 2½" wide strip. Attach to bottom of joined blocks; see general reference diagram.

Joining the Rows

1. Refer to the general reference diagram as a guide to the order for joining rows together.
2. Measure your quilt top at this stage; it should be a 48½" square.

INNER SASHING

1. From each of turquoise and pink fabric cut one 1½" strip totalling 48½" and one totalling 50½" in length (you will probably need to join smaller lengths).
2. Sew shorter turquoise strip to left side of quilt and pink to right.
3. Sew longer turquoise strip to top of quilt and pink to bottom.

PIECED BORDERS

1. From left over fabrics cut 52 squares of fabric, each measuring 5¼" x 5¼" and 4 rectangles measuring 2½" x 4½" (used for the centres of the borders).
2. From the squares of fabric make 52 quarter square blocks (see General Techniques).
3. Join 4" squares and rectangles together to make border strips:
   - 2 x 6 squares each side of a rectangle for sides
   - 2 x 7 squares each side of a rectangle for top and bottom
4. Sew shorter strips onto each side of quilt.
5. Sew longer strips to top and bottom of quilt.

OUTER SASHING

1. From each of turquoise and pink fabric cut one 1½" strip totalling 58½" and one totalling 60½" in length (you will probably need to join smaller lengths).
2. Sew shorter pink strip to left side of quilt and turquoise to right.
3. Sew longer pink strip to top of quilt and turquoise to bottom.

QUILTING

1. Prepare the quilt sandwich. If you plan to have your quilting done on a Long Arm machine ensure that your backing is at least 3" larger all round than your quilt top (I suggest at least 67" x 67") or size as requested by your machinist.
2. Baste and quilt according to your personal preference.

'Down on the Farm' was custom long arm quilted. The outside edges of the animals and main landscape features, plus the main background seams were 'stitched in the ditch'. The individual animals were not quilted, thereby allowing them to 'stand forward' of the background. The background areas were quilted using a variety of appropriate quilting patterns.

The sashings and borders were simply 'stitch in the ditch' quilted. Appropriate variegated threads were used with a complementary colour on the back.

BINDING

1. Trim all sides of quilt so that layers are even and corners are square.
2. My quilt is edged with a ½" double binding. Cut sufficient 3" wide strips of fabric such that, when joined, they will go around the edge of the quilt, plus about 10" extra in length.
3. Join all strips together on the diagonal to make a single long strip.
4. Fold binding strip in half along the entire length, right sides outermost. Press.
5. Fold in ¼" along length of open long edge (both layers together). Press.
6. Starting at centre of bottom edge and with right sides together, pin binding in place so that the ¼" fold line lies ½" in from the edge (you may find it useful to mark this line). Pin in place. Machine stitch along this fold line until ½" from the corner. Backstitch a little and remove quilt from the machine. Fold the binding strip up at 45° and then back down such that the ¼" fold line now lies ½" in from the next quilt edge. This gives spare fabric to fold over to the back of the quilt, ensuring neat corners.
7. Stitch along fold line, starting from top edge and thereby holding the mitre, fold in place as you sew.
8. Continue sewing down the binding strip and forming corners until you return to the start. Fold in overlap edges to form a neat ending. Slip stitch down.
9. Fold the binding to the back of the quilt, carefully easing out fullness at corners. Pin.
10. Hem along the seam line. Sew down mitred corners.

FINISHING TOUCHES

1. Add button eyes and appropriate tails.
2. Embroider any additional features etc. as indicated in the relevant block instructions.
3. Don't forget to add that all-important label.

Two by Two

Based on the story of Noah's Ark, 'Two by Two' makes the perfect companion design to 'Down on the Farm' and is also available as a foundation pieced pattern booklet.

Please contact me via my website:

www.lesleybrankinquilts.co.uk

or send an SAE to the address given on the inside cover for current price and ordering information.

Quarter Square Triangle Block (makes 2)

1. Take two contrasting squares of fabric and place them right sides together.
2. Using a pencil, draw a line on the wrong side of one square (the lightest is usually the easiest to see) from one corner to its opposite diagonal corner (A to D).
3. Draw another line across the other diagonal (B to C).
4. Using a ¼" sewing machine foot* stitch either side of the A to D diagonal.

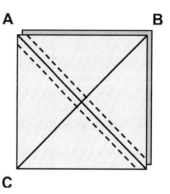

*If you do not have a ¼" sewing foot then measure a line each side of the diagonal and stitch along these.

5. Cut along the B to C diagonal and **then** cut along the A to D diagonal to give four pairs of co-joined triangles; these will make two Quarter Square Triangle blocks.
6. Press seams to one side (same side for each pair).
7. With right sides facing, abut seams together.
8. Take two triangle pairs and place right sides together, sew along the longer side using a ¼" seam allowance. Repeat for other pair.
9. Press seams open.

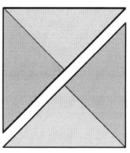

Plaited Tail

1. Take 6 strands of perlé thread, each about 7" long.
2. Fold in half and stitch centre fold firmly to animal's bottom.
3. Divide the strands into three and plait for a length of about 2", knot end securely and trim.

The tail can either be left to hang free or stitched down.

Tassel Tail

1. Take 4 strands of perlé thread, each about 8" long.
2. Fold in half and stitch centre fold firmly to animal's bottom.
3. Bring the attaching thread round the tail to bind individual strands together.
4. Trim ends evenly.

FOUNDATION PIECING - A BRIEF GUIDE

Foundation Piecing, also known variously as 'Paper Piecing' and the 'Stitch and Flip Technique', is a very accurate piecing technique where fabric patches are stitched to the reverse of a foundation block or unit (part of a block). Depending on the material used for the foundation, this can be either left permanently in place (e.g. lightweight cotton fabric or sew-in interfacing) or can be removed (e.g. paper or Stitch 'n' Tear).

The advantages of Foundation Piecing over the use of traditional piecing or template methods is that it allows you greater scope to piece more intricate designs. It can also be very quick to work once you become familiar with the technique.

Materials

You will need:
- Foundation paper, Stitch 'n' Tear or fine fabric e.g. calico or lawn
- Cottons or other fine fabrics e.g. silk
- Neutral coloured sewing thread

General Method

Patches are stitched to the blank side of the foundation. As such it is useful to have access to a light source (e.g. window or light box) to help position patches. Seam allowances are trimmed to size as the block is stitched so accurate cutting of the pieces is not necessary. When machine stitching, remember to use a slightly smaller stitch than usual especially if the foundation is to be removed.

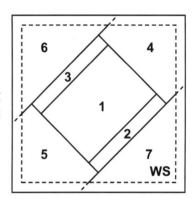

Foundation Template

First, the block or unit design must be traced or photocopied accurately on to the foundation and the order of stitching each patch noted. The design should appear in reverse to that of the finished block or unit.

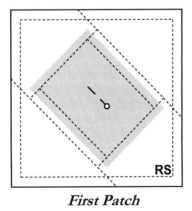

First Patch

Begin with the patch for area 1. Cut a piece of fabric slightly larger than the area to be covered and position this right side up, onto the blank side of the foundation covering area 1. Pin in place.

Next cut a piece of fabric that generously covers area 2. Place this right side down over patch 1, aligning the corresponding allowance edge. To help with placement of fabric, mark each end of the stitching line with a pin. Pin patch 2. Turn the foundation over and stitch along the line between patch 1 and 2 starting and finishing a few stitches beyond the marked line.

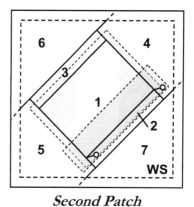

Second Patch

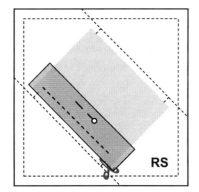

Trim Fabric Allowance

Turn unit over and trim seam allowances.

Flip patch 2 so that the right side of the fabric is now visible and press flat.

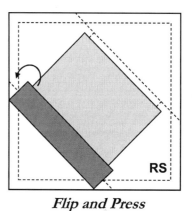

Flip and Press

Trim unit allowance to ¼"

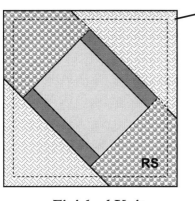

Finished Unit

Continue to stitch patches in numerical order, making sure that the fabric extends over the seam allowance around the outer edge of the unit. When the unit is complete, trim back seam allowances to a neat ¼".

Sewing Units Together

Units are sewn together with a ¼" seam allowance as they would be for any traditionally pieced patchwork technique. If units are different shapes then follow the construction order given in the instructions.

Papers need to be removed - this can be done once a unit has been trimmed to its accurate size or it can be done after units have been joined.

Fabric foundations can be left in if desired.

BULL

Block Size: 6" x 6" (make 1)

You will need:

- background - pale grey
- bull - brown, light brown, black
- buttons - 2 x ³⁄₈" black
- perlé thread - black

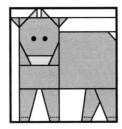

Making a Block

1. Copy Foundation Units A through D.
2. Foundation piece Units A, B, D and E using pale grey for background.
3. (Optional) - To give the bull 'hooves' first join strips of black and body fabric together and use this for pieces 1b, 3b, 5b and 7b when making Unit C.
4. Foundation piece Unit C using pale grey for background.
5. Referring to Unit Placement diagram, join Unit A to B, then add Unit C and finally Unit D.
6. Sew Unit E to the top of the sub-block.

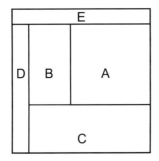

Unit Placement
(right sides facing)

7. Trim finished block to 4½" x 4½".
8. Remove papers (can be done before or after trimming).

Finishing (completed after quilting)

1. Sew on buttons for eye.
2. Using black perlé thread, make a ***plaited tail***. Attach.

CAT

Block Size: 4" x 4" (make 2)

You will need:

- background - pale blue or pale green
- cat - orange/tan or black/white
- button - 1 x ¼" green or brown

Making a Block

1. Copy Foundation Units A through E, optionally reversing the pattern for the second cat.
2. Foundation piece Units A through E using either pale blue of pale green for background.
3. Referring to Unit Placement diagram, join Unit B to A and then add these to Unit C.
4. Join Unit D to Unit E and then attach to A-C sub block.
5. Cut a 4½" x ¾" strip of background fabric (Unit F) and sew this to the side of the cat sub-block.

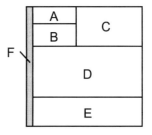

Unit Placement
(right sides facing)

6. Trim finished block to 4½" x 4½".
7. Remove papers (can be done before or after trimming).

Finishing (completed after quilting)

1. Sew on button for eye.
2. Embroider whiskers (optional).

COCKEREL

Block Size: 4" x 4" (make 1)

You will need:
- background - pale grey
- cockerel - brown, beige, mottled brown, green, red, orange,
- button - 1 x ¼" black

Making a Block

1. Copy Foundation Units A through G.
2. Foundation piece Units A through G using pale grey for background.
3. Referring to Unit Placement diagram, join Unit A to B and then attach Unit C.
4. Join Unit D to Unit E and then attach to A-C sub block.
5. Join Unit F to Unit G. Add to bottom of cockerel sub block.
6. Cut a 4½" x 1" strip of background fabric (Unit H) and sew this to the right of the cockerel sub-block as shown.

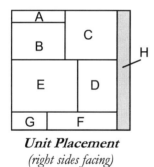

Unit Placement
(right sides facing)

7. Trim finished block to 6½" x 6½".
8. Remove papers (can be done before or after trimming).

Finishing (completed after quilting)

1. Sew on button for eye.

> ### TIP
> *Reduce the machine stitch length when foundation piecing.*
>
> *This makes it easier to remove the papers afterwards.*

COLLIE DOG

Block Size: 5" x 5" (make 2)

You will need:
- background - pale green
- dog – black, white
- button - 1 x ¼" brown or black

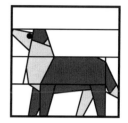

Making a Block

1. Copy Foundation Units A through F, optionally reversing the pattern for the second dog.
2. Foundation piece Units A through F using pale green for background.
3. Referring to Unit Placement diagram, join Unit B to A.
4. Attach Unit D to E and then add C, followed by F.
5. Join to A-B sub block.
6. Cut a 5½" x 1½" strip of background fabric (Unit G) and sew this to the top of the sub-block.

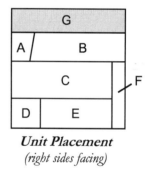

Unit Placement
(right sides facing)

7. Trim finished block to 5½" x 5½".
8. Remove papers (can be done before or after trimming).

Finishing (completed after quilting)

1. Sew on button for eye.
2. Embroider whiskers (optional).

COW

Block Size: 6" x 6" (make 3)

You will need:

- background - pale blue or pale grey
- cow - black/white print or brown, pink, black
- buttons - 2 x ⅜" black
- perlé thread - black

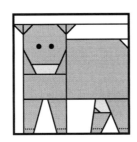

Making a Block

1. Copy Foundation Units A through D.
2. Foundation piece Units A, B and D using pale blue or pale grey for background.
3. (Optional) - To give the cow 'hooves' first join strips of black and body fabric together and use this for pieces 3b, 5b, 7b and 9b when making Unit C.
4. Foundation piece Unit C using appropriate colour for background.
5. Referring to Unit Placement diagram, join Unit A to B and then attach Unit C. Finally, attach Unit D.
6. Cut a 6½" x 1" strip of background fabric (Unit E) and sew this to the top of the cow sub-block.

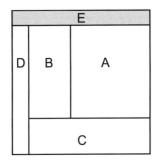

Unit Placement
(right sides facing)

7. Trim finished block to 6½" x 6½".
8. Remove papers (can be done before or after trimming).

Finishing (completed after quilting)

1. Sew on buttons for eyes.
2. Using black perlé thread, make a ***plaited tail***. Attach.

DONKEY

Block Size: 6" x 6" (make 2)

You will need:

- background - pale blue or pale green
- donkey - medium or dark grey, pink, black
- button - 1 x ⅜" black
- perlé thread - black

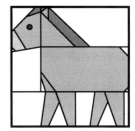

Making a Block

1. Copy Foundation Units A through D.
2. Foundation piece Units A through C using pale blue or pale green for background.
3. (Optional) - To give the donkey 'hooves' first join strips of black and body fabric together and use this for pieces 2b, 4b, 6b and 8b when making Unit D.
4. Foundation piece Unit C using appropriate colour for background.
5. Referring to Unit Placement diagram, join Unit A to B and then attach Unit C. Finally, attach Unit D.

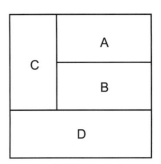

Unit Placement
(right sides facing)

6. Trim finished block to 6½" x 6½".
7. Remove papers (can be done before or after trimming).

Finishing (completed after quilting)

1. Sew on button for eye.
2. Using black perlé thread, make a ***plaited tail***. Attach.
3. Embroider a nostril using a French knot. (Optiional)

DRAKE

Block Size: 3" x 4" (make 2))

You will need:
- background - pale blue
- drake - brown, light brown, orange, white, green
- button - 1 x ¼" black

Making a Block

1. Copy Foundation Units A through D, optionally reversing the pattern for one of the drakes.
2. Foundation piece Units A through D using pale blue for background.
3. Referring to Unit Placement diagram, join Unit A to B and then attach Unit C. Finally, attach Unit D.

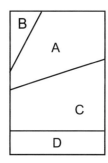

Unit Placement
(right sides facing)

4. Trim finished block to 3½" x 4½".
5. Remove papers (can be done before or after trimming).

Finishing (completed after quilting)

1. Sew on button for eye.

DUCK

Block Size: 3" x 4" (make 3)

You will need:
- background - pale blue
- duck - brown, light brown, orange
- button - 1 x ¼" black

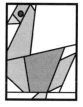

Making a Block

1. Copy Foundation Units A through C, optionally reversing the pattern for two ducks.
2. Foundation piece Units A, B and C using pale blue for background.
3. Referring to Unit Placement diagram, join Unit A to B and then attach Unit C.

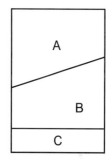

Unit Placement
(right sides facing)

4. Trim finished block to 3½" x 4½".
5. Remove papers (can be done before or after trimming).

Finishing (completed after quilting)

1. Sew on button for eye.

TIP

Before removing papers score along stitching lines with the back of a stitch ripper.

This makes it easier to remove the papers afterwards.

GOAT

Block Size: 5" x 5" (make 2)

You will need:
- background - pale grey
- goat - beige or grey, white
- button - 1 x ¼" black

Making a Block

1. Copy Foundation Units A through F.
2. Foundation piece Units A, B, C and D using pale grey for background.
3. Referring to Unit Placement diagram, join Unit B to A, then add C. Finally, attach Unit D.
4. Foundation piece Units E and F using pale grey for background.
5. Referring to Unit Placement diagram, join Units E and F. Join these together and add to the previous Units.
6. Cut a 5" x 1¼" strip of background fabric (Unit G) and sew this to the top of the goat sub-block.
7. Cut a 5½" x 1" strip of background fabric (Unit H) and sew this to the side of the goat sub-block.

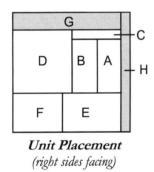

Unit Placement
(right sides facing)

8. Trim finished block to 5½" x 5½".
9. Remove papers (can be done before or after trimming).

Finishing (completed after quilting)

1. Sew on button for eye.

GOOSE

Block Size: 3" x 4" (make 5)

You will need:
- background - pale green
- goose - tan, 2 shades cream
- buttons - 1 x ¼" black

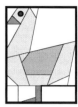

Making a Block

1. Copy foundation Units A through C.
2. Foundation piece Units A, B and C using pale green for background.
3. Referring to Unit Placement diagram, join Unit A to B. Attach Unit C.

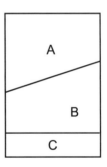

Unit Placement
(right sides facing)

4. Trim finished block to 3½" x 4½".
5. Remove papers (can be done before or after trimming).

Finishing (completed after quilting)

1. Sew on button for eye.

TIP

Press and trim seam allowances each time a new piece is added to a block.

This assists with ensuring accuracy and reduces unnecessary bulk.

HEN

Block Size: 3" x 3" (make 4)

You will need:
- background - pale grey
- hen - brown, beige, red, orange
- button - 1 x ¼" black

Making a Block

1. Copy Foundation Units A through C, optionally reversing the pattern for one hen.
2. Foundation piece Units A, B and C using pale grey for background.
3. Referring to Unit Placement diagram, join Unit A to B. Attach Unit C.

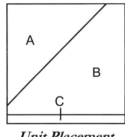

Unit Placement
(right sides facing)

4. Trim finished block to 3½" x 3½".
5. Remove papers (can be done before or after trimming).

Finishing (completed after quilting)

1. Sew on button for eye.

TIP

Audition unusual fabrics as possible candidates for inclusion in blocks.

Only small scraps are needed - are there any interesting textures that can be incorporated?

HILLS & FARMER

Block Size: 7" x 14" (make 1)

You will need:
- hills - sky blue, grass green, hill green,
- farmer – grass green, greens, pink, browns
- buttons - 2 x ¼"

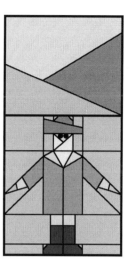

Making the Hills Block

1. Copy Foundation Unit A.
2. Foundation Piece Unit A.
3. Remove papers and trim block to 7½" x 6½".

Making the Farmer Block

1. Copy Foundation Units A through H.
2. Use grass green for background throughout.
3. Foundation piece Units A through C.
4. Referring to Unit Placement diagram join these together.

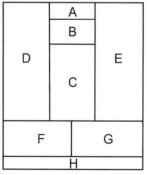

Unit Placement
(right sides facing)

5. Foundation piece Units D and E. Attach to central sub unit.
6. Foundation piece units F through H. Join Units F and G and then attach to Unit H.
7. Remove papers and trim finished block to 7½" x 8½".
8. Join to Hills Block.

Finishing (completed after quilting)

1. Sew on buttons for eyes.

HORSE

Block Size: 6" x 6" (make 2)

You will need:

- background - pale grey
- horse - browns
- button - 1 x ⅜" black
- perlé thread - brown

Making a Block

1. Copy Foundation Units A through D.
2. Foundation piece Units A through C using pale grey for background.
3. (Optional) - To give the ~~zebra~~ horse 'hooves' first join strips of black and striped fabric and use this for pieces 2b, 4b, 6b and 8b when making Unit D.
4. Foundation piece Unit D again using pale grey for background.
5. Referring to Unit Placement diagram, join Unit A to B and then add Unit C. Finally, attach Unit D.

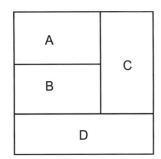

Unit Placement
(right sides facing)

6. Trim finished block to 6½" x 6½".
7. Remove papers (can be done before or after trimming).

Finishing (completed after quilting)

1. Sew on button for eye.
2. Using brown perlé thread, make a ***tassel tail***. Attach.

HOUSE & PATH

Block Size: 7" x 14" (make 1)

You will need:

- house - sky blue, hill green, creams, red, greys, purple
- path - grass green, cream
- button - 1 x ⅜" brown (door handle)

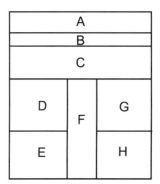

Making the Path Block

1. Copy foundation Unit A.
2. Using grass green as the background, Foundation Piece Unit A.
3. Remove papers and trim block to 7½" x 6½".

Making the House Block

1. Copy Foundation Units A through H.
2. Foundation piece Units A through C using hill green and sky as shown.
3. Referring to Unit Placement diagram join these together.

Unit Placement
(right sides facing)

4. Foundation piece Units D through H.
5. Join Units D to E and G and H and then attach either side of Unit F as shown.
6. Remove papers and trim finished block to 7½" x 8½".
7. Join to Path Block.

Finishing (completed after quilting)

1. Sew on a button for door handle.

PIG

Block Size: 5" x 5" (make 3)

You will need:

- background - pale blue and pale green
- pig - fabric - 2 shades pink, black
- buttons - 2 x ⅜" black, 2 x ¼" tan
- perlé thread - pink

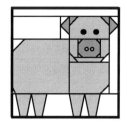

Making a Block

1. Copy Foundation Units A through E, optionally making a mirrored image for the second block.
2. Foundation piece Units A through D using pale blue and green for backgrounds.
3. (Optional) - To give the pig trotters, first join strips of black and pink fabrics and use for pieces 2p, 4p, 6p and 8p when making Unit E.
4. Foundation piece Unit E using appropriate colour for background.
5. Referring to Unit Placement diagram, join Unit A to Unit B and then add Unit C. Finally attach Unit D.

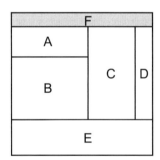

Unit Placement
(right sides facing)

6. Attach Unit E to the bottom.
7. Cut a 5½" x 1" strip of background fabric (Unit F) and sew this to the top.
8. Trim finished block to 5½" x 5½".
9. Remove papers (can be done before or after trimming).

Finishing (completed after quilting)

1. Sew on buttons for eyes and snout.
2. Using stem stitch and pink perlé thread, embroider a curly tail.

RABBIT

Block Size: 3" x 3" (make 2)

You will need:

- background - pale green
- rabbit - brown, beige, white
- button - 1 x ¼" black

Making a Block

1. Copy Foundation Units A through D, optionally reversing the pattern for the second rabbit.
2. Foundation piece Units A, B, C and D using pale green for background.
3. Referring to Unit Placement diagram, join Unit B to A and C to D. Join these together.

Unit Placement
(right sides facing)

4. Cut a 3½" x 1½" strip of background fabric (Unit E) and sew this to the top of the rabbit sub-block.
5. Trim finished block to 3½" x 3½".
6. Remove papers (can be done before or after trimming).

Finishing (completed after quilting)

1. Sew on button for eye.
2. Embroider whiskers (optional).

SHEEP

Block Size: 5" x 5" (make 7)

You will need:
- background - pale green, blue and grey
- sheep - curly 'wool', black, cream
- buttons - 2 x ⅜" black

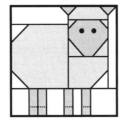

Making a Block

1. Copy Foundation Units A through D, optionally reversing the pattern for some of the sheep.
2. Foundation piece Units A through C using pale green, blue or grey for background.
3. (Optional) - To give the sheep 'feet' first join strips of black and cream fabric and use for pieces 2b, 3b, 5b and 7b when making Unit D.
4. Foundation piece Unit D using appropriate colour for background.
5. Referring to Unit Placement diagram, join Units A and C to either side of Unit B.

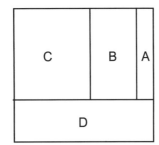

Unit Placement
(right sides facing)

6. Finally add Unit D to the bottom.
7. Trim finished block to 5½" x 5½".
8. Remove papers (can be done before or after trimming).

Finishing (completed after quilting)

1. Sew on buttons for eyes.

TURKEY

Block Size: 4" x 4" (make 2)

You will need:
- background - pale blue or pale green
- turkey - brown, beige, white, red, orange
- buttons - 2 x ¼" black

Making a Block

1. Copy Foundation Units A through D.
2. Foundation piece Units A, B, C and D using pale blue or pale green for background.
3. Referring to Unit Placement diagram, join Unit B to A and C to A. Finally attach Unit D.

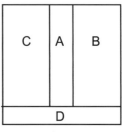

Unit Placement
(right sides facing)

4. Trim finished block to 4½" x 4½".
5. Remove papers (can be done before or after trimming).

Finishing (completed after quilting)

1. Sew on buttons for eyes.

> **TIP**
> *Remove papers in the opposite numerical order to that used for sewing i.e. remove the last piece first.*
>
> *This makes it much easier to remove papers fully.*

Old MacDonald had a farm,
E-I-E-I-O.
And on that farm he had some sheep,
E-I-E-I-O.
With a "baa baa" here and a "baa baa" there,
here a "baa", there a "baa", everywhere a "baa baa".
Old MacDonald had a farm,
E-I-E-I-O.

Old MacDonald had a farm,
E-I-E-I-O.
And on that farm he had some cows,
E-I-E-I-O.
With a "moo moo" here and a "moo moo" there,
here a "moo", there a "moo", everywhere a "moo moo".
Old MacDonald had a farm,
E-I-E-I-O.

etc.   *(a traditional nursery rhyme)*

23

Old MacDonald had some . . .

Goats

Sheep

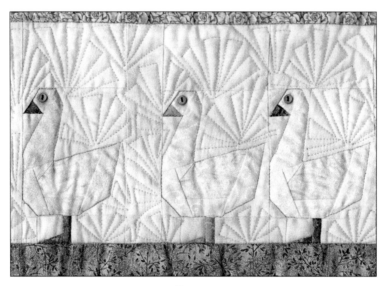

Geese

Cats

Dogs

24

and some . . .

Cows

(& a Bull)

Ducks & Drakes

Horses

Donkeys

and some . . .

Pigs

Turkeys

Hens

Rabbits

(& a Cockerel)

Bull - Unit E

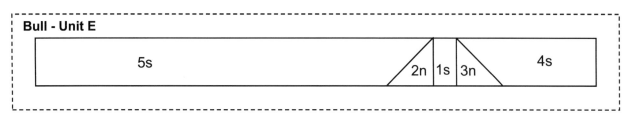

5s | 2n | 1s | 3n | 4s

Bull - Unit D

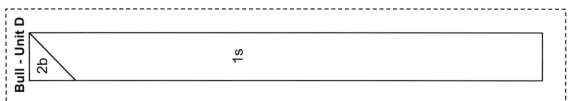

2b | 1s

Bull - Unit B

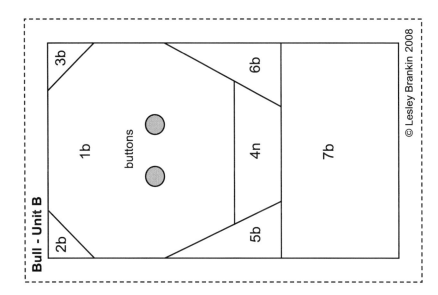

3b

1b

buttons

6b

2b

4n

5b

7b

© Lesley Brankin 2008

BULL BLOCK
(make 1)
Foundation papers
(reversed ready for piecing)

Fabric Key
b: body
n: nose/horns
s: sky

Bull - Unit A

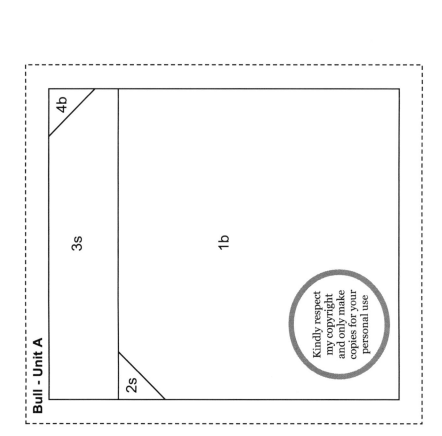

4b

3s

1b

2s

Kindly respect
my copyright
and only make
copies for your
personal use

Bull - Unit C

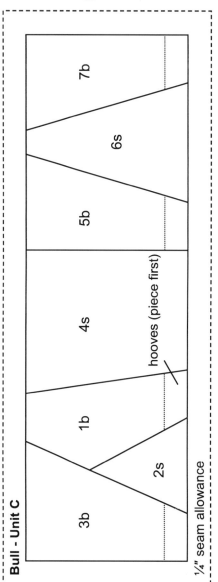

7b

6s

5b

4s

hooves (piece first)

3b

1b

2s

¼" seam allowance

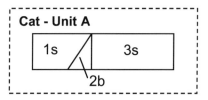

Cat - Unit A

1s   3s   2b

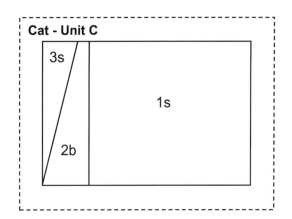

Cat - Unit C

3s   1s   2b

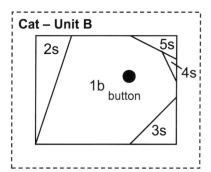

Cat – Unit B

2s   5s   4s   1b button   3s

Fabric Key
b: body
c: contrast
s: sky

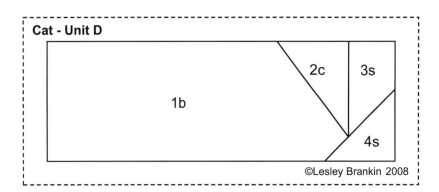

Cat - Unit D

1b   2c   3s   4s

©Lesley Brankin 2008

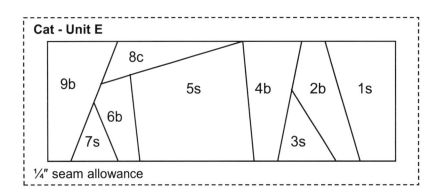

Cat - Unit E

9b   8c   5s   4b   2b   1s   6b   7s   3s

¼" seam allowance

CAT BLOCK
(make 2 - 1 reversed)
Foundation papers
(reversed ready for piecing)

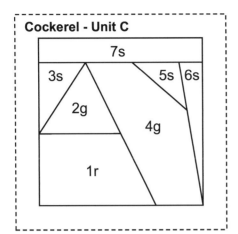

Cockerel - Unit C

7s · 3s · 2g · 4g · 5s · 6s · 1r

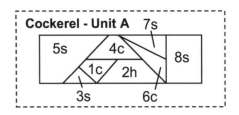

Cockerel - Unit A

5s · 4c · 7s · 1c · 2h · 8s · 3s · 6c

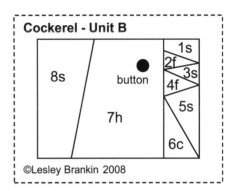

Cockerel - Unit B

8s · button · 7h · 1s · 2f · 3s · 4f · 5s · 6c

©Lesley Brankin 2008

Fabric Key
b: body
h: head
r: red feathers
g: green feathers
f: foot/beak
w: wing
c: comb/wattle
s: sky

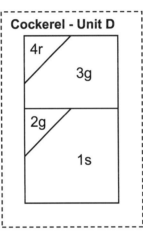

Cockerel - Unit D

4r · 3g · 2g · 1s

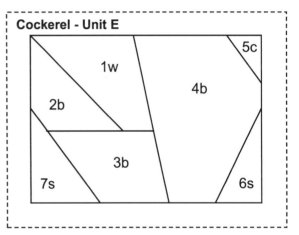

Cockerel - Unit E

1w · 5c · 2b · 4b · 3b · 7s · 6s

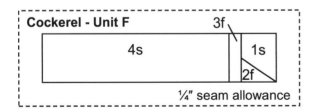

Cockerel - Unit F

4s · 3f · 1s · 2f

¼" seam allowance

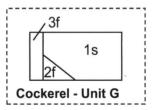

3f · 1s · 2f

Cockerel - Unit G

COCKEREL BLOCK

(make 1)

Foundation papers

(reversed ready for piecing)

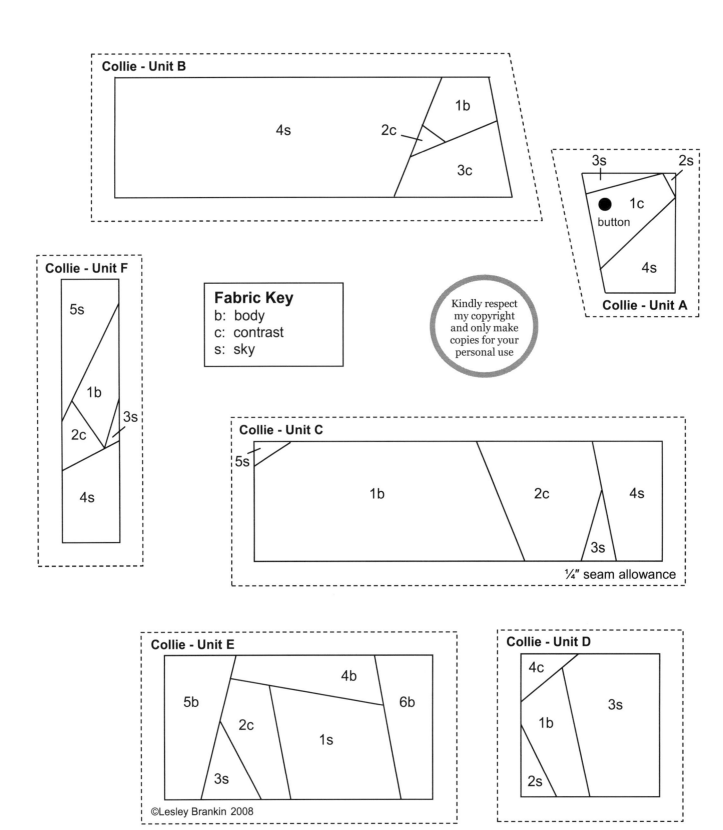

COLLIE DOG BLOCK

(make 2 - 1 reversed)
Foundation papers
(reversed ready for piecing)

Fabric Key
b: body
n: nose/udder
s: sky

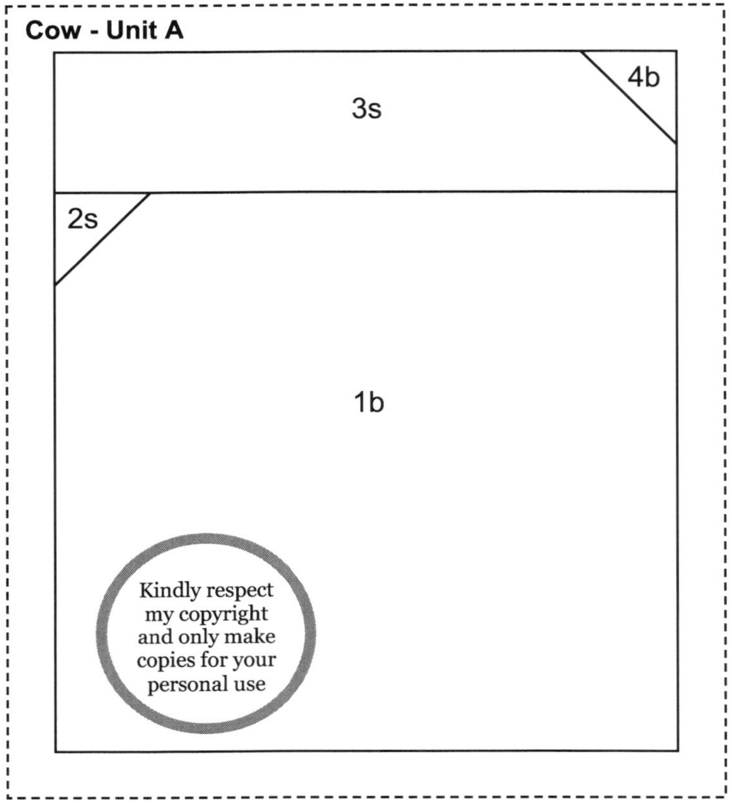

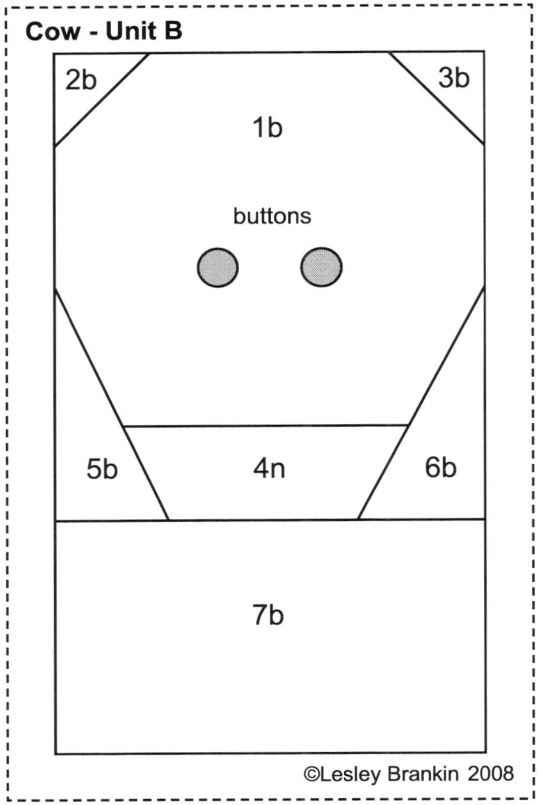

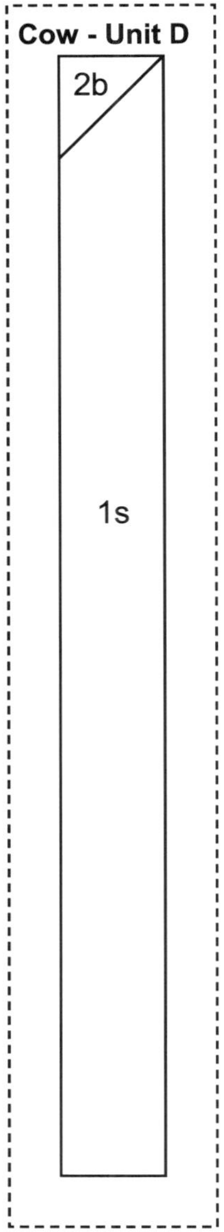

COW BLOCK
(make 3)
Foundation papers
(reversed ready for piecing)

©Lesley Brankin 2008

Cow - Unit D

2b

1s

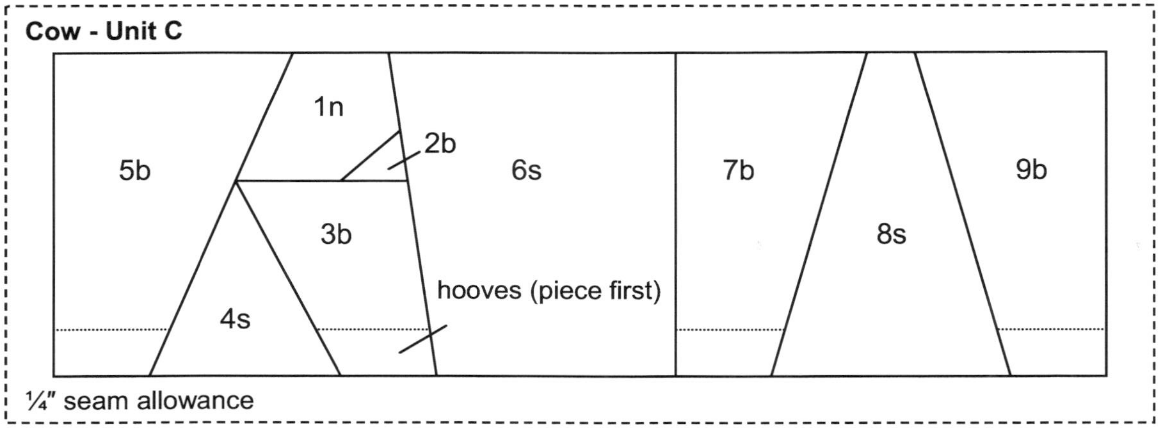

Cow - Unit B

3b

1b

buttons

6b

2b

4n

5b

7b

Cow - Unit A

4b

3s

1b

2s

Cow - Unit C

9b

8s

7b

2b

6s

1n

3b

hooves (piece first)

5b

4s

¼" seam allowance

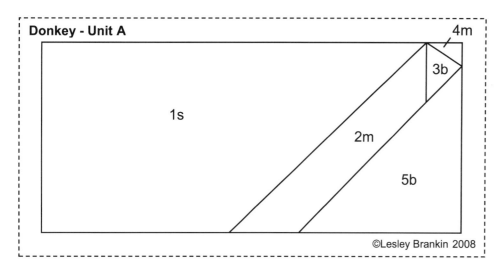

Donkey - Unit A

1s

2m

3b

4m

5b

©Lesley Brankin 2008

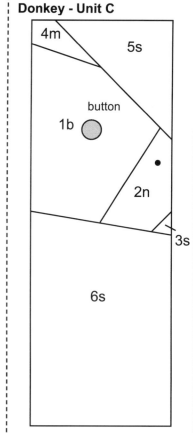

Donkey - Unit C

4m

5s

button

1b

2n

3s

6s

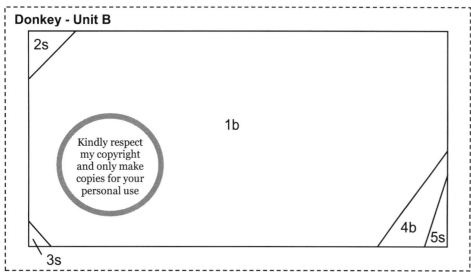

Donkey - Unit B

2s

1b

Kindly respect my copyright and only make copies for your personal use

3s

4b

5s

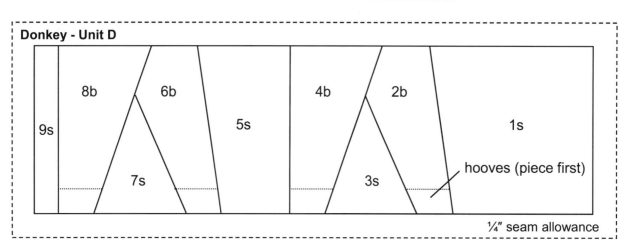

Donkey - Unit D

9s

8b

6b

5s

7s

4b

2b

1s

3s

hooves (piece first)

¼" seam allowance

DONKEY BLOCK

(make 2)

Foundation papers

(reversed ready for piecing)

Fabric Key

b: body
n: nose
m: mane
s: sky

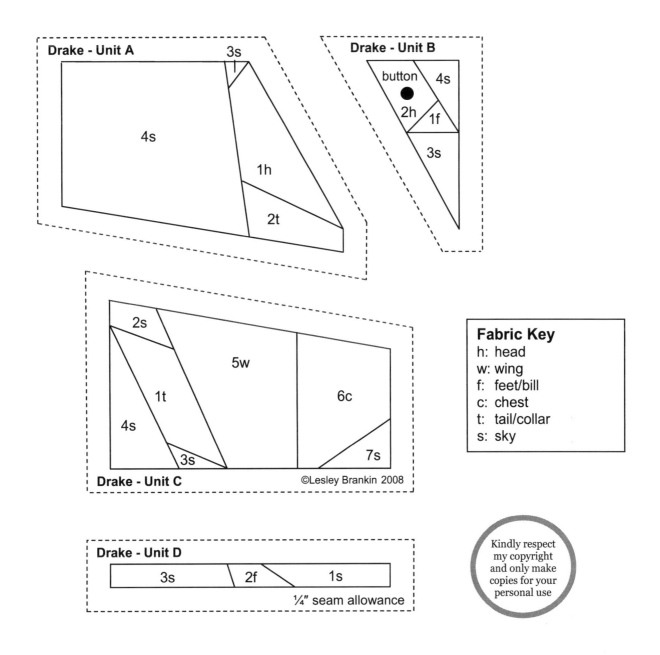

Fabric Key
h: head
w: wing
f: feet/bill
c: chest
t: tail/collar
s: sky

©Lesley Brankin 2008

¼" seam allowance

DRAKE BLOCK
(make 2 - 1 reversed)
Foundation papers
(reversed ready for piecing)

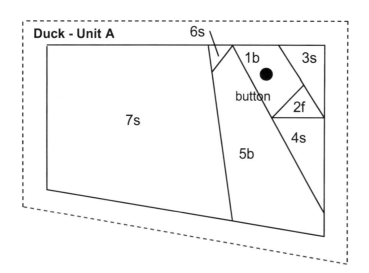

Duck - Unit A

6s

1b · button

3s

2f

4s

7s

5b

Fabric Key
b: body
w: wing
f: feet/bill
s: sky

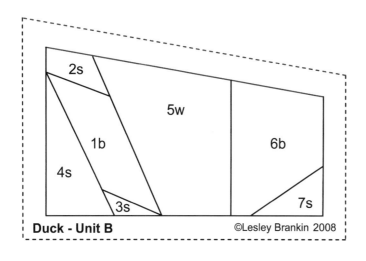

2s

5w

1b

6b

4s

3s

7s

Duck - Unit B   ©Lesley Brankin 2008

DUCK BLOCK

(make 3 - 2 reversed)
Foundation papers
(reversed ready for piecing)

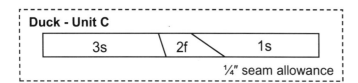

Duck - Unit C

3s   2f   1s

¼" seam allowance

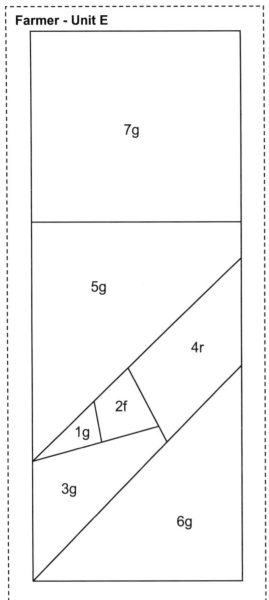

Farmer - Unit E

7g

5g

4r

2f

1g

3g

6g

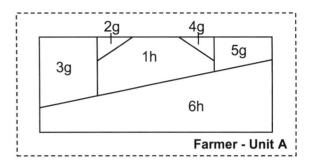

2g 4g

3g

1h

5g

6h

Farmer - Unit A

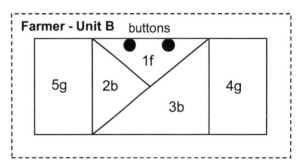

Farmer - Unit B buttons

5g

2b

1f

3b

4g

Farmer - Unit C

6g

2c

1b

3c

7g

4r

5r

©Lesley Brankin 2008

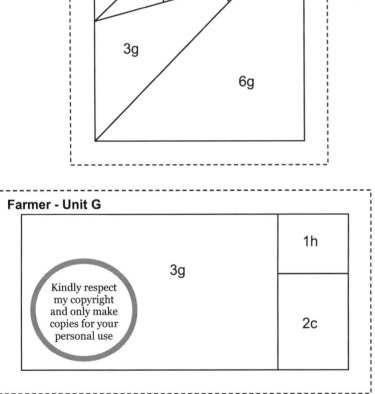

Farmer - Unit G

1h

3g

Kindly respect
my copyright
and only make
copies for your
personal use

2c

FARMER (page 1 of 2)

(make 1)

Foundation papers

(reversed ready for piecing)

Fabric Key

c: collar & boots
f: face & hands
h: hat & trousers
b: beard
r: robe
g: grass

35

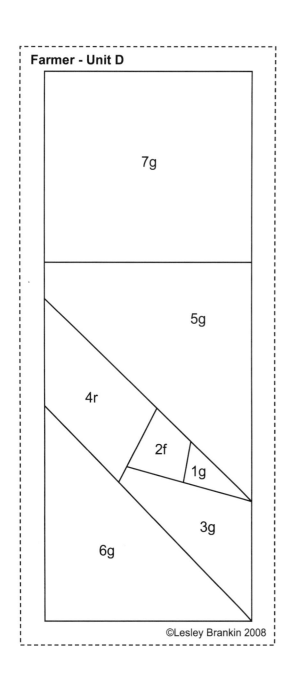

Farmer - Unit D

7g

5g

4r

2f

1g

3g

6g

©Lesley Brankin 2008

Fabric Key
c: collar & boots
f: face & hands
h: hat & trousers
b: beard
r: robe
g: grass

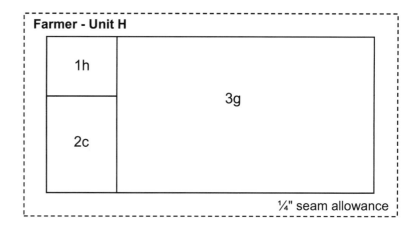

Farmer - Unit H

1h

2c

3g

¼" seam allowance

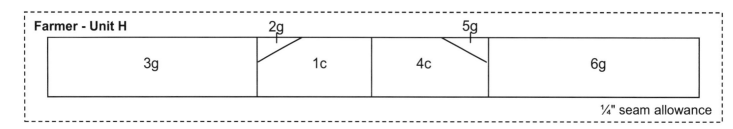

Farmer - Unit H

3g

2g

1c

5g

4c

6g

¼" seam allowance

FARMER (page 2 of 2)
(make 1)
Foundation papers
(reversed ready for piecing)

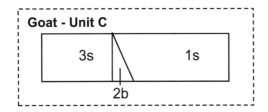

Goat - Unit C

3s   2b   1s

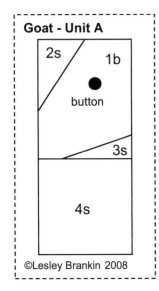

Goat - Unit A

2s   1b
button
3s
4s

©Lesley Brankin 2008

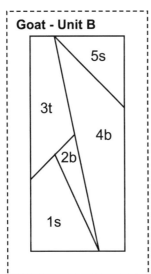

Goat - Unit B

5s
3t
4b
2b
1s

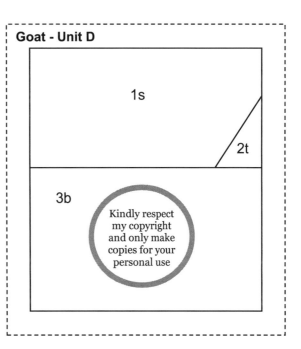

Goat - Unit D

1s   2t

3b

Kindly respect
my copyright
and only make
copies for your
personal use

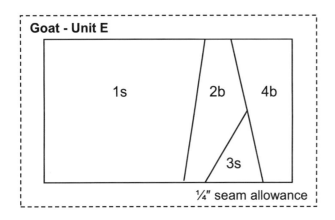

Goat - Unit E

1s   2b   4b
3s

¼" seam allowance

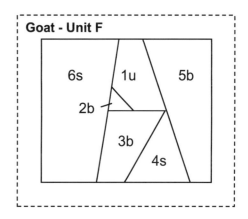

Goat - Unit F

6s   1u   5b
2b
3b
4s

GOAT BLOCK

(make 2)

Foundation papers
(reversed ready for piecing)

Fabric Key
b: goat
t: tail/ear
u: udder
s: sky

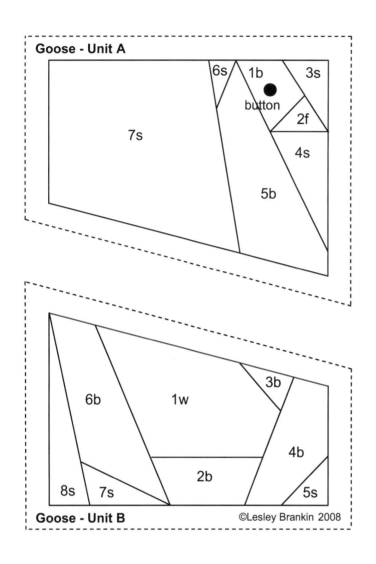

Goose - Unit A

6s 1b 3s

● button

7s 2f

4s

5b

Goose - Unit B

6b 1w 3b

4b

2b

8s 7s 5s

©Lesley Brankin 2008

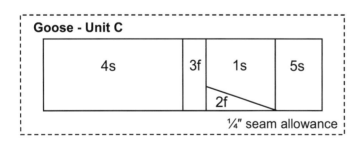

Goose - Unit C

4s 3f 1s 5s

2f

¼" seam allowance

Fabric Key
b: body
w: wing
f: feet/bill
s: sky

Kindly respect
my copyright
and only make
copies for your
personal use

GOOSE BLOCK
(make 5)
Foundation papers
(reversed ready for piecing)

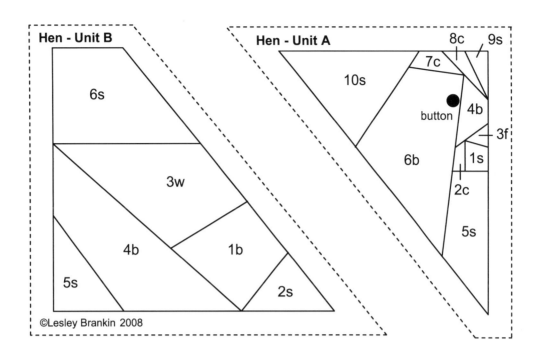

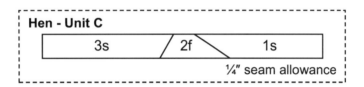

Fabric Key
b: body
f: foot/beak
w: wing
c: comb/wattle
s: sky

Kindly respect
my copyright
and only make
copies for your
personal use

HEN BLOCK
(make 4 – 1 reversed)
Foundation papers
(reversed ready for piecing)

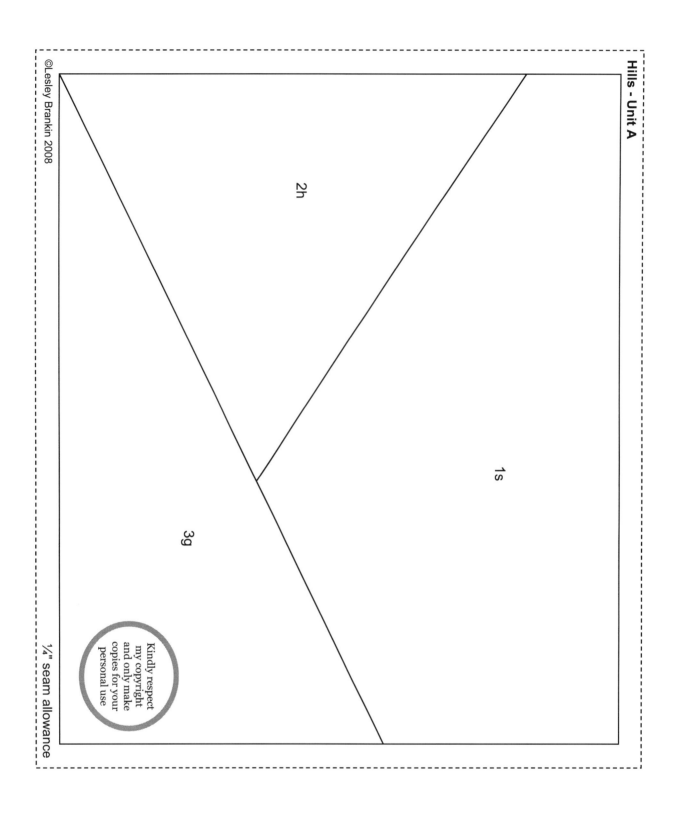

©Lesley Brankin 2008

¼" seam allowance

2h

1s

3g

Kindly respect
my copyright
and only make
copies for your
personal use

Fabric Key
h: hill
g: grass
s: sky

HILLS
(make 1)
Foundation papers
(reversed ready for piecing)

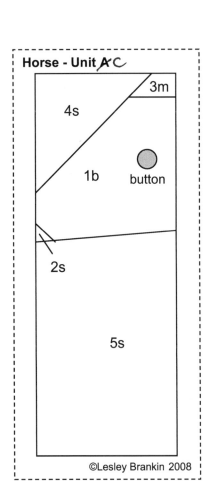

Horse - Unit A̶ C

3m

4s

1b

button

2s

5s

©Lesley Brankin 2008

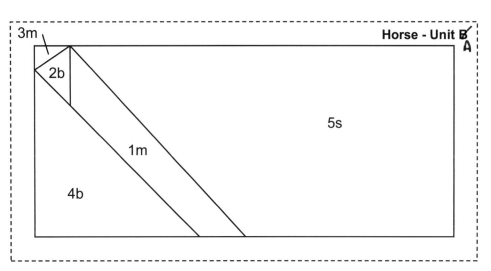

3m

Horse - Unit B̶ A

2b

5s

1m

4b

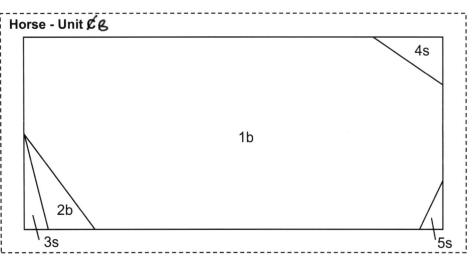

Horse - Unit C̶ B

4s

1b

2b

3s

5s

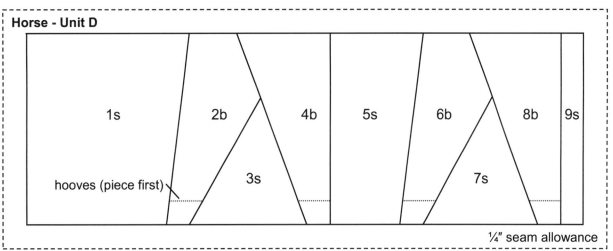

Horse - Unit D

1s

2b

4b

5s

6b

8b

9s

hooves (piece first)

3s

7s

¼" seam allowance

Kindly respect my copyright and only make copies for your personal use

Fabric Key
b: body
m: mane
s: sky

HORSE BLOCK
(make 2)
Foundation papers
(reversed ready for piecing)

41

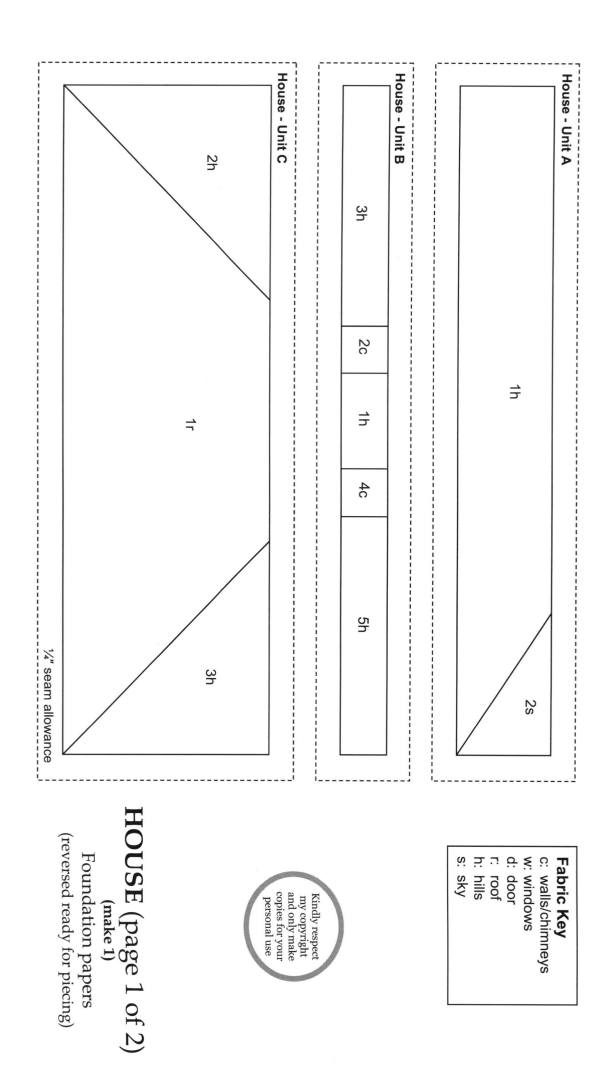

House - Unit A

1h

2s

House - Unit B

3h 2c 1h 4c 5h

House - Unit C

2h

1r

3h

¼" seam allowance

Fabric Key
c: walls/chimneys
w: windows
d: door
r: roof
h: hills
s: sky

Kindly respect
my copyright
and only make
copies for your
personal use

HOUSE (page 1 of 2)
(make 1)
Foundation papers
(reversed ready for piecing)

HOUSE (page 2 of 2)
(make 1)
Foundation papers
(reversed ready for piecing)

Fabric Key
c: walls/chimneys
w: windows
d: door
r: roof
h: hills
s: sky

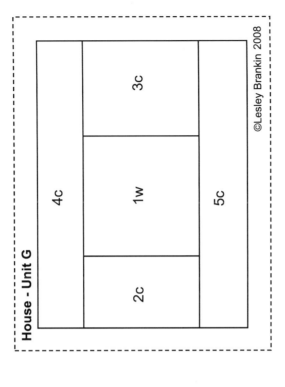

House - Unit G

4c 1w 3c 2c 5c

©Lesley Brankin 2008

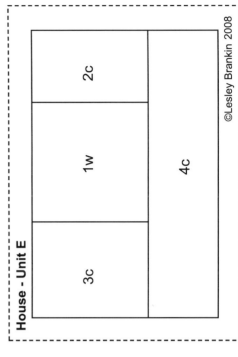

House - Unit E

3c 1w 2c 4c

©Lesley Brankin 2008

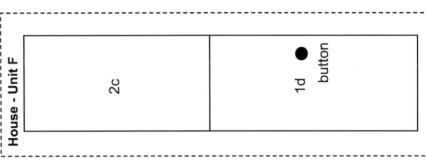

House - Unit F

2c 1d button

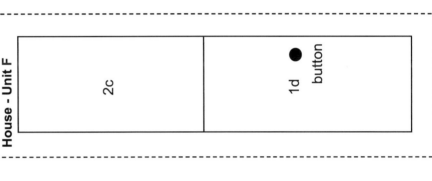

House - Unit D

2c 4c 1w 3c 5c

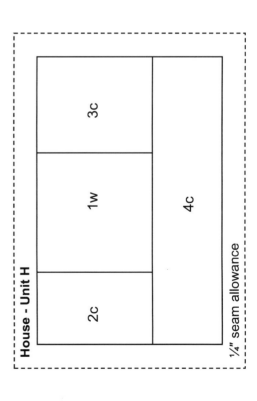

House - Unit H

2c 1w 3c 4c

¼" seam allowance

43

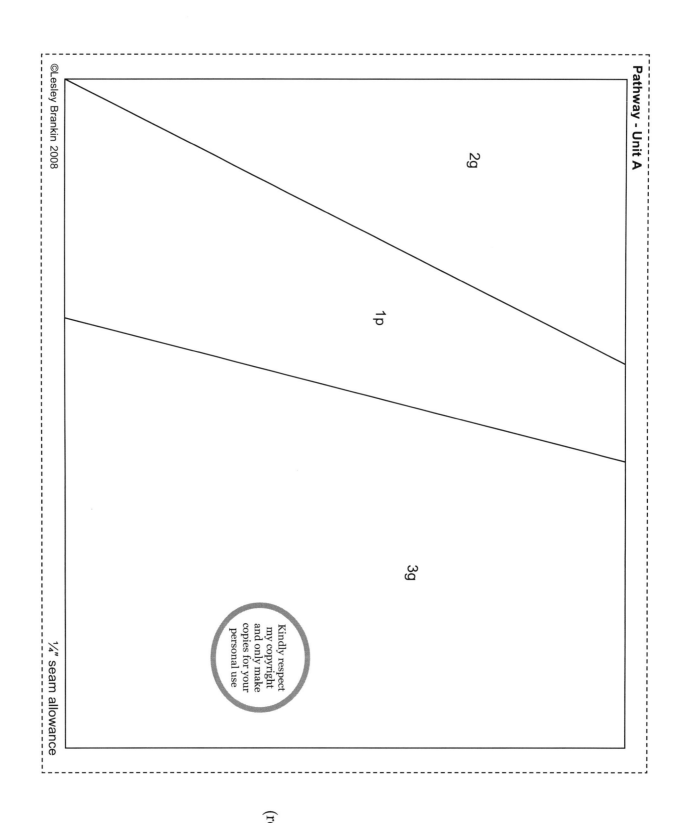

©Lesley Brankin 2008

2g

1p

3g

Kindly respect
my copyright
and only make
copies for your
personal use

¼" seam allowance

Fabric Key
g: grass
p: pathway

PATHWAY
(make 1)
Foundation papers
(reversed ready for piecing)

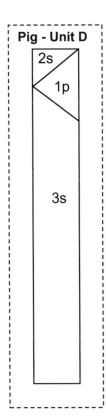

Pig - Unit D

2s
1p
3s

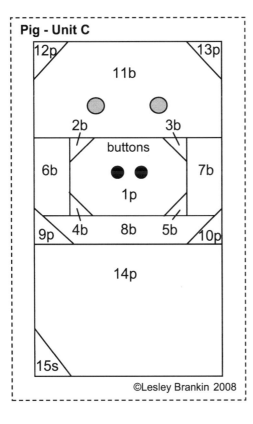

Pig - Unit C

12p   11b   13p

2b   3b

buttons

6b   7b

1p

9p   4b   8b   5b   10p

14p

15s

©Lesley Brankin 2008

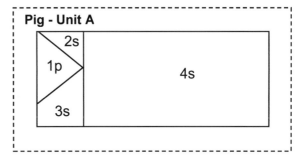

Pig - Unit A

2s
1p
4s
3s

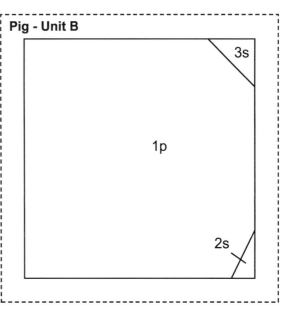

Pig - Unit B

3s

1p

2s

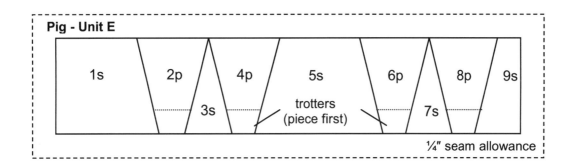

Pig - Unit E

1s   2p   4p   5s   6p   8p   9s

3s   trotters
(piece first)   7s

¼" seam allowance

PIG BLOCK

(make 3)

Foundation papers
(reversed ready for piecing)

Fabric Key
b: face
p: body, ears, legs
s: sky

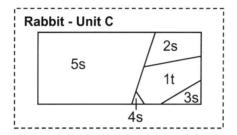

Rabbit - Unit C

2s
5s
1t
3s
4s

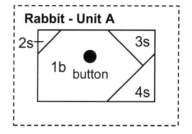

Rabbit - Unit A

2s
3s
1b
button
4s

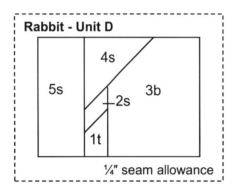

Rabbit - Unit D

4s
5s
3b
2s
1t

¼" seam allowance

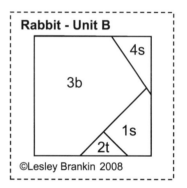

Rabbit - Unit B

4s
3b
1s
2t

©Lesley Brankin 2008

RABBIT BLOCK

(make 2 - 1 reversed)

Foundation papers
(reversed ready for piecing)

Kindly respect my copyright and only make copies for your personal use

Fabric Key
b: body
t: tail /ear/foot
s: sky

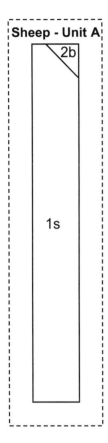

Sheep - Unit A

2b

1s

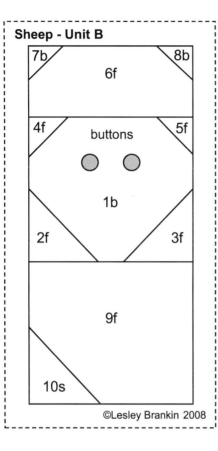

Sheep - Unit B

7b

6f

8b

4f

buttons

5f

1b

2f

3f

9f

10s

©Lesley Brankin 2008

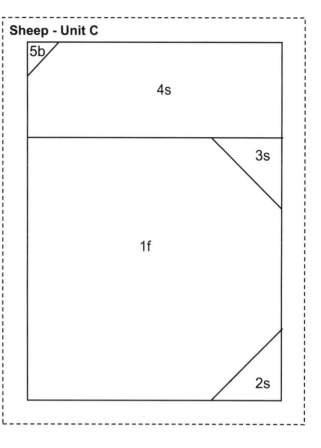

Sheep - Unit C

5b

4s

3s

1f

2s

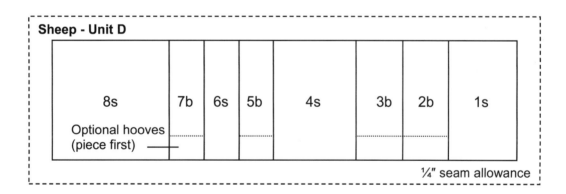

Sheep - Unit D

| 8s | 7b | 6s | 5b | 4s | 3b | 2b | 1s |

Optional hooves
(piece first)

¼" seam allowance

SHEEP BLOCK

(make 7 - reverse 2)

Foundation papers
(reversed ready for piecing)

Fabric Key
b: face, legs, ears
f: fleece
s: sky

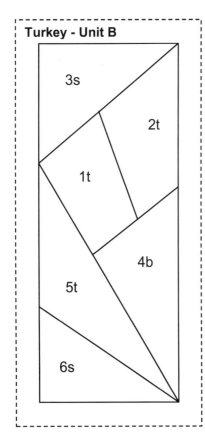

Turkey - Unit B

3s
2t
1t
4b
5t
6s

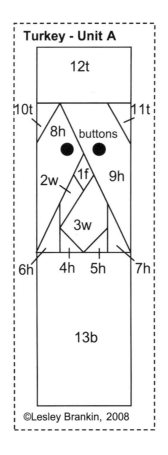

Turkey - Unit A

12t
10t
8h
buttons
11t
2w
1f
9h
3w
6h
4h
5h
7h
13b

©Lesley Brankin, 2008

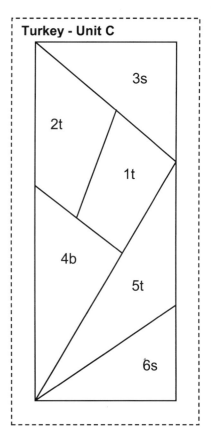

Turkey - Unit C

3s
2t
1t
4b
5t
6s

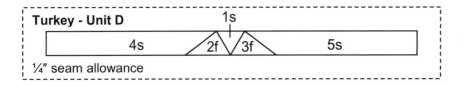

Turkey - Unit D

1s
4s
2f
3f
5s

¼" seam allowance

TURKEY BLOCK

(make 2)
Foundation papers
(reversed ready for piecing)

Fabric Key	
b:	body
f:	feet/beak
h:	head
t:	tail
w:	wattle
s:	sky